TALKING ABOUT

Drugs

Sarah Levete

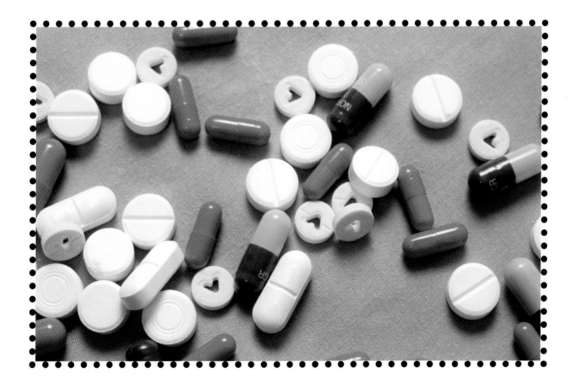

Franklin Watts
London • Sydney

© Aladdin Books Ltd 2004

Designed and produced by
Aladdin Books Ltd
28 Percy Street
London W1T 2BZ

First published in Great Britain in 2004 by
Franklin Watts
96 Leonard Street
London EC2A 4XD

ISBN: 0 7496 5510 0

Design:
Flick, Book Design and Graphics

Picture research:
Brian Hunter Smart

Editor:
Jim Pipe

The consultant, David Uffindall, is a
Drugs Education Consultant with a
Local Education Authority.

The publishers would like to
acknowledge that the photographs
reproduced in this book have been
posed by models or have been
obtained from photographic agencies.

A CIP record for this book is available
from the British Library.

Contents

4   Why should I know about drugs?

6   What is a drug?

8   What about drugs from a doctor?

10   How are medicines used the wrong way?

12   What are illegal drugs?

14   What do drugs do?

16   What are the risks of using drugs?

18   Why do people take drugs?

20   Do all drug users have a drugs problem?

22   How can I say "no" to drugs?

24   How do drug users affect others?

26   Why can it be hard to give up drugs?

28   What if someone I know takes drugs?

30   What can I do?

31   Find Out More

32   Index

"Why should I know about drugs?"

You may have heard confusing things about drugs. Some people say that drugs kill. Others say that drugs from a doctor save lives. Both are right. Drugs such as medicines can help people get better. But other drugs, including illegal drugs, can be harmful and can even kill people. So too can medicines and alcohol, if not used properly.

Drugs are all around you. They include the caffeine in coffee, the alcohol in beer and the chemicals in medicines.

This book helps to answer your questions about drugs. It tells you about the effect drugs can have on a person's body and life.

Understanding the issues will help you make clear and safe choices as you grow up.

Did you know...

Drugs mean different things to different people. To a drug dealer, illegal drugs are a way to make money. To a doctor, drugs can save the lives of patients. A drug inhaler to help control asthma (left) is helpful as long as the patient follows the doctor's instructions. But all drugs, including medicines, can be dangerous if taken the wrong way.

"What is a drug?"

Like food, drugs are taken into the body. They can change the way your body works and how you behave.

Drugs come in many forms, such as pills, creams, or liquids, some of which are injected with a needle. Some are swallowed, like the medicine you may take to fight an illness. Others are breathed in, such as inhalants.

Everyday drugs include alcohol and the nicotine in tobacco. The caffeine in some soft drinks can make you more alert or make sleeping difficult.

What you put into your body changes how it works. The sugar in chocolate can give you a short burst of energy.

Think about it

Powerful drugs that help control illness or help deal with depression are only available on prescription from the doctor. Other drugs can be bought from a chemist, such as painkillers to help ease a headache.

Illegal drugs, such as speed or ecstasy, are obtained from a dealer. These drugs change the way a person feels but have no medical benefit.

Some illegal drugs, such as cannabis, are made from plants. Others, such as ecstasy, are made from chemicals. Medical drugs are made from plants or chemicals to a safe and tested formula, unlike illegal drugs.

A person using illegal drugs is never sure what the drug is made of or how strong it is. What looks like cannabis (below) could actually be dried animal dung!

"What about drugs from a doctor?"

If you are unwell, the doctor may prescribe a drug to help you get better. Sometimes people need to take drugs from the doctor for a long time in order to stay alive. However, even drugs from a doctor can be harmful.

Drugs from the doctor can help you recover from an illness.

If a person takes too much medicine, he or she may become seriously ill. If the patient doesn't finish the course of medicine, the illness is unlikely to clear up.

Because medical drugs are made to a carefully controlled formula, a person can be told how much to take and for how long.

Did you know...

Doctors are trained to understand the effect a drug can have on a person. Getting the right drug in the correct dose (the amount of medicine) for a person is a skilled job.

• A child should only take medicine when a responsible grown-up is present.

• Only ever take the dose recommended by the doctor or on the packet or bottle.

• Never take someone else's medicine. What is ok for one person could be harmful for another.

• Follow any instructions that come with a medicine. All drugs, including medicines, can have side-effects.

"How are medicines used the wrong way?"

When we feel sad, a nice surprise or a treat can help to cheer us up. But when some people feel unhappy, they need to take medical drugs to change how they feel.

These drugs are only given by doctors to patients with a medical need. But people can get hold of them illegally. They abuse the drugs, which means using them the wrong way.

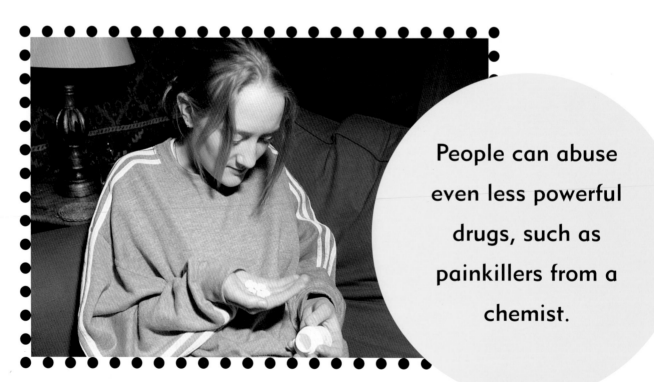

People can abuse even less powerful drugs, such as painkillers from a chemist.

Some athletes abuse drugs such as steroids to make themselves stronger, even though there is no medical need. Steroids can do a lot of damage to the user's body.

If an athlete's drug abuse is found out, he or she may be banned from sporting events for many years.

Did you know...

You may have heard of "glue-sniffing". Glues and lighter fuel are types of solvents. They are not meant to be used as drugs, but some people breathe or sniff them to feel "high". But trying to get this short rush of feeling can also lead to cold sores, being sick or even death.

"What are illegal drugs?"

You may have heard people talking about illegal drugs. Illegal means "against the law", and people are not allowed to own or sell these drugs. Because illegal drugs are not tested like medicines, no one can ever be sure what is in them. This means that people who use an illegal drug can never be sure how the drug will affect them.

Illegal drugs are also known as street drugs because many dealers sell them on the streets.

As well as official names, street drugs have nicknames, such as snow, E or whizz. They make different changes to the body. Some make the user feel relaxed.

Other drugs make the person feel full of energy. All illegal drugs can damage a user's body, and some will do it quicker than others. Class A drugs are the most powerful.

Did you know...

COCAINE – Class A
A white powder that is snorted (sniffed in) or injected. This drug can be very addictive and can cause chest and heart problems. Crack cocaine is smoked. It can make users violent and is highly addictive.

HEROIN – Class A
A white powder that is injected or snorted. This drug is very addictive. Taking too much (overdosing) can lead to death. Sharing needles can also lead to dangerous infections such as HIV/AIDS.

LSD – Class A
Tiny tablets or squares of paper that are swallowed. LSD changes the way users experience the world, called "tripping". Bad trips can be very frightening or lead to mental health problems.

ECSTASY – Class A
Tablets that are swallowed. Using ecstasy can cause kidney, liver and heart problems, tiredness and depression. Ecstasy has been linked with brain damage. It also dehydrates the user, which means it removes fluids from the body. Drinking too much water to try to replace this lost fluid can be as risky as not drinking enough.

AMPHETAMINES – Class B
A grey or white powder. These drugs can cause anxiety or panic and may make some users feel tired and depressed.

CANNABIS – Class C
This drug can come in brown lumps known as resin, or leaves (grass). It is usually smoked, often with tobacco. Because of this, users can become addicted to cigarettes. Smoking cannabis over many years can cause memory loss or a lack of energy.

"What do drugs do?"

People may misuse a particular drug for the effect they hope it will have on their mind or body. But the effect depends on the drug, its strength, who uses it and the place in which it is used.

For instance, a young man injecting heroin by himself could die if he injects too much and there is no one to get help. One girl taking LSD could feel alright, but her friend may have a terrifying experience.

Drugs may make a person feel happy. But they can also cause illness, accidents, and in some cases, death.

Using some drugs can create a change of mood for some people, creating a "high" or feeling of well-being. But the same drug can have the opposite effect on others.

The long-term effects can be more serious. They range from pale, spotty skin to brain damage or heart attacks.

Think about it

Regularly using drugs can change a person's body and mind so much that he or she wants more and more of them. We say they are "addicted" to drugs. The person may be unable to function without using drugs. They may do almost anything to get hold of them, including stealing or using violence.

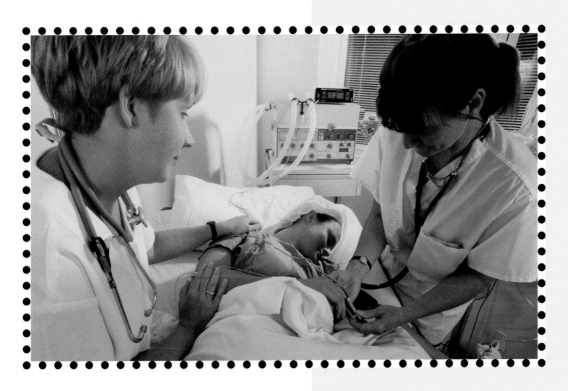

"What are the risks of using drugs?"

You may have overheard someone saying how much they enjoy taking drugs. But anyone who misuses drugs risks damaging their mind and body, especially if they take them often. If they use dirty needles to inject drugs they can also risk getting infections such as hepatitis or HIV. Smoking tobacco or illegal drugs can lead to lung cancer, even years after a person has stopped smoking.

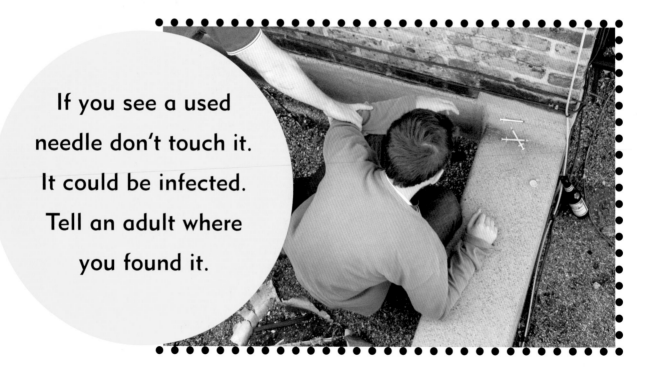

If you see a used needle don't touch it. It could be infected. Tell an adult where you found it.

Street drugs can muddle and cloud a person's judgement. It is more likely for someone on drugs to have an accident, especially if they are near such places as railways, rivers or roads, or if they are driving.

Mixing different drugs or drugs and alcohol is very dangerous because it is hard to know the combined effect of the drug cocktail. Taking too much of a drug can lead to physical collapse or even death.

Think about it

If someone uses illegal drugs, they also risk getting into trouble. Drug dealers often use violence to deal with users who cannot pay them for the drugs they have used.

Being caught with illegal drugs, sharing them or selling them can lead to a fine, a criminal record and even time in prison.

"Why do people take drugs?"

You may wonder why people take drugs with all the risks. But ask a parent why they or their friends drink alcohol or smoke. They may say they like the taste or the way it makes them feel.

People often try street drugs to get a "high", or just to see what it feels like. Some may start using drugs to rebel against their parents.

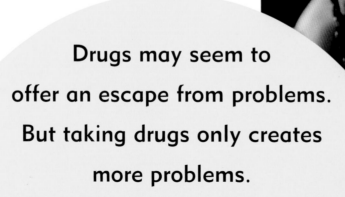

Drugs may seem to offer an escape from problems. But taking drugs only creates more problems.

Drugs change the way a person feels, so a person facing problems at school or at home may turn to drugs as a way to escape the difficult feelings. But drugs don't make problems disappear, and they can often cause even more difficult ones.

Some people take drugs such as ecstasy to make a night-out seem more fun. But the after-effects can include feeling panicked or depressed, or even mental illness.

Did you know…

At some time, you will probably meet people who use drugs. You may feel under pressure to try drugs to show that you are as cool as your mates. Your friends may make you feel silly if you don't try. But think about the possible consequences. It's your life that is at stake. Making a wise, responsible and healthy choice will leave you in control. If your friends won't accept that, are they worth it?

"Do all drug users have a drugs problem?"

You have probably heard people say that all drugs are bad. But if you see people enjoying a drink or smoking cannabis, you may wonder what is so bad about them.

Drugs cause problems when people take risks. The more you understand about them, the safer you will be.

Everyone who uses drugs runs a risk of developing a health problem or an addiction.

For instance, some people think that sniffing glue a few times won't be a problem. But they may not realise that the first time some people sniff glue it can make them black out and may even kill them.

Regularly using drugs also creates a need. To start with, a person may think he or she is in control. But soon they find that they want the drug more and more.

Street drugs are particularly risky because no one knows their strength. It is easy to take too much – and they can kill.

My Story

"My big sister started trying drugs to fit in with her friends. She started off taking a pill now and then. Soon she was taking them every day – she had become addicted. It took her a long time to come off them, and it's been really hard on all of us." Sam

"How can I say 'no' to drugs?

No one can make you take drugs, though some people may try to persuade you. But you can say no to them. It's not always an easy thing to do, but it is a good choice.

If you are offered drugs, think about yourself rather than what others may think. To help you stand up for yourself and your life, the following tips may help:

It's your life, and it's your decision. Don't let others decide for you.

① Avoid situations where others put pressure on you.

② If someone offers you drugs, be aware of how dangerous they can be. It is up to you to keep your mind and body safe.

③ Look the other person in the eye, be confident and say "No" firmly.

④ If someone is putting you under pressure, why not practise these replies. Say clearly, "I prefer to stay in control", or, "I don't want to take a chance on a drug, especially if no one knows what it is really in it."

⑤ Remember, you can always ask advice from a grown-up that you trust.

Think about it

Involve yourself with friends who share your interests and make you feel good about yourself for who you are. Join a club or get involved in an activity that you enjoy. There are many ways to have fun with friends without taking drugs.

"How do drug users affect others?"

It is not just drug users who are affected by drugs. It is all of the people around them at home, at school or at work.

People who regularly use drugs may feel the need for the drug so much that they cannot think about anything else. They may not care that they are ruining others' lives as well as their own.

The people closest to a person with a drug problem suffer the most.

Drugs cost a lot of money. If someone needs to spend a lot of money on drugs it means they may get into financial difficulty. They may even lose their home. Children playing in an area where people use drugs could hurt themselves on needles with which drug users have injected drugs. The children could even catch a serious infection from the needles.

My story

"I've always been really close to my big sister Lisa. But then she started taking drugs. She says they make her feel good, but I think they just make her lose control. I've even seen her attacking her friends. She's also stealing from Mum to pay for them. I'm really worried about Lisa, but she won't listen. It is really upsetting me." Ronan

"Why can it be hard to give up drugs?"

Young people who try drugs may think it is easy to stop taking them. If they are lucky, they may try a drug once or twice and find they can stop without much difficulty.

But many drugs are addictive. Regular drug users can find it very hard to give up. It can be very painful as their body has to get used to being without the drug.

Coming off drugs is hard work. But in time, people can start to live and enjoy their lives again.

Even when people have come off drugs, they have to learn to deal with problems without depending on drugs to escape.

Some drug users have to avoid meeting people and going to places where they may be tempted to misuse drugs again. They may even have to leave their home and friends and start a new life somewhere else.

Did you know...

People coming off drugs need a lot of support. Their families may need support, too. There are many sources of help. Self-help groups run by former drug users offer addicts encouragement and understanding. Some people may need drugs from the doctor to help handle the painful symptoms of giving up drugs.

"What if someone I know takes drugs?"

If someone close to you is using drugs, and it is affecting you, talk to a grown-up you trust, such as a teacher or parent.

Letting someone know about another person with a drug problem is not telling tales and could save someone's life.

Telling someone about a person's drug abuse could save a life.

If you are being put under pressure from people around you to take drugs, tell a grown-up you trust. They will be understanding and will help you stand up for yourself. If you are tempted by drugs, think about what you are doing and the risks you might be taking. Talk to someone you trust to find the support you may need.

Think about it

A lot of people are tempted to take drugs. Some do so without serious problems. For others, it can ruin their lives and those of their families. Talking to someone about drug abuse can help the person with the problem and those around them.

"What can I do?"

• Unless you are ill, you do not need drugs. If you eat and sleep well, your body can usually look after itself.

• It's how people use drugs that causes problems. Medical drugs can fight illness, but they can also cause addiction and even death if they are abused.

• Choose friends and activities that don't involve drugs.

• If people offer you drugs, think about the risks, not just the short-term feelings the drugs may give. Be clear about your choice to say "No", and feel good about it.

Enjoy life without the problems that drugs can cause.

31

Books on drugs

If you want to read more about drugs, try:

The *My Healthy Body* series by
Jen Green (Franklin Watts)
Choices and Decisions: Taking Drugs by
Pete Sanders & Steve Myers (Franklin Watts)
Learn to say no: Solvents/Cannabis
by Angela Royston (Heinemann)

Contact information

If you want to talk to someone who doesn't
know you, these organisations can help:

Drugscope
32-36 Loman Street, London SE1 0EE
A 24-hour free helpline: 0800 77 66 00
Information line: 08707 743 682
Email: info@drugscope.org.uk
Website: www.drugscope.org.uk

Release
388 Old Street
London EC1V 9LT
Tel: 020 7729 9904
Email: info@release.org.uk
Website: www.release.org.uk

UK National Drugs Helpline
Tel: 0800 77 66 00

On the Web

These websites are also helpful:

www.d-2k.co.uk
www.thesite.org
www.famanon.org.uk
www.trashed.co.uk
www.ukna.org
www.adanz.org.nz

Australian Drug
Foundation
409 King Street,
West Melbourne,
VIC 3003
PO Box 818 North
Melbourne VIC 3051
Phone: 03 9278 8100
Email: adf@adf.org.au
Website: www.adf.org.au

Alcohol Drug Association
New Zealand (ADA)
Support for anyone involved in drug misuse
PO Box 13-496, First Floor , 215 Gloucester St
Christchurch, New Zealand
Tel: 03 379 8626   Helpline: 0800 787 797,
Email: ada@adanz.org.nz

There is lots of useful information about drugs on the internet.

Index

accidents 14, 17
addiction 13, 15, 20, 21, 26, 30

doctors 4, 5, 7, 8, 9, 10
drugs
  different types 6, 7, 13
  on prescription 7, 8, 9
  risks 11, 13, 14, 15, 16, 17, 18, 19,
    21, 25

effect of drugs
  on behaviour 6, 13, 14, 17, 25
  on body 6, 11, 13, 15, 16, 17, 19,
    21
  on health 5, 8, 9, 13, 15, 16, 17, 20
  on mind 11, 13, 14, 15, 16, 19
  on others 24, 25

everyday drugs
  alcohol 4, 6, 17, 18, 20
  caffeine (in coffee/soft drinks) 4, 6
  nicotine (in tobacco) 6, 16, 18

getting help 26, 27, 28, 29, 31

giving up drugs 21, 26, 27
glue-sniffing 11, 21

helplines 31

illegal (street) drugs 4, 5, 6, 7, 12, 13,
    17, 18, 21
  cannabis 7, 13
  ecstasy 7, 13, 19
  heroin 13, 14
  LSD 13, 14
infections 16, 25

laws on drugs 20

making choices 5, 19, 20, 21, 22, 23, 30
medicines (medical drugs) 4, 5, 6, 7, 8,
    9, 12
misusing medicines 10, 11, 30
  painkillers 7, 10
  steroids 11

saying "no" 22, 23, 30
solvents 11

Photocredits

Abbreviations: l-left, r-right, b-bottom, t-top, c-centre, m-middle
All photos supplied by PBD except for:
Front cover, 3tr, 3mr, 5bl — Select Pictures. 1, 5tr, 7tl, 15b — Corbis. 2 — Brand X Pictures. 3br, 18r, 19b — Image 100. 4 — Flat Earth. 7br — US Department of Justice; DEA. 9tl, 23br, 30r — Photodisc. 10bl, 12b, 26b, 27b, 28b — Roger Vlitos. 11tl — Corel. 14r, 20r, 25br — Image State.